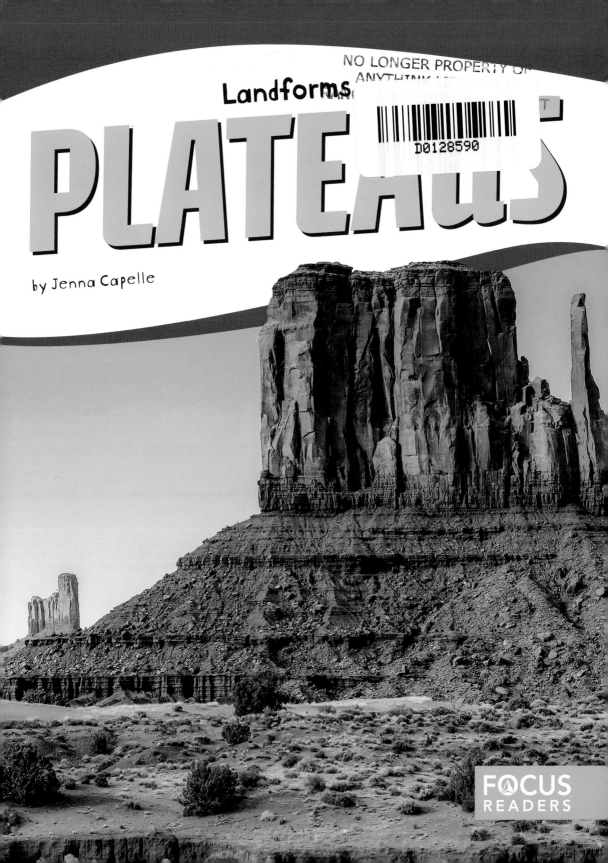

Landforms

PLATEAUS

by Jenna Capelle

FOCUS
READERS

FOCUS READERS

www.focusreaders.com

Focus Readers is distributed by North Star Editions:
sales@northstareditions.com | 888-417-0195

Produced for Focus Readers by Red Line Editorial.

Photographs ©: lucky-photographer/iStockphoto, cover, 1; Yani/Shutterstock Images, 4–5; Jam Norasett/Shutterstock Images, 7; Philip Schubert/Shutterstock Images, 8–9; GuilhermeMesquita/Shutterstock Images, 11, 29; Weather500/Shutterstock Images, 13; Martinez de la Varga/Shutterstock Images, 14–15; Animeah/Shutterstock Images, 16–17; Tyler Hulett/Shutterstock Images, 18; Andrew Mayovskyy/Shutterstock Images, 21; Serg Zastavkin/Shutterstock Images, 22–23; Taesik Park/Shutterstock Images, 25; kavram/Shutterstock Images, 27

ISBN
978-1-63517-896-8 (hardcover)
978-1-63517-997-2 (paperback)
978-1-64185-200-5 (ebook pdf)
978-1-64185-099-5 (hosted ebook)

Library of Congress Control Number: 2018931695

Printed in the United States of America
Mankato, MN
May, 2018

About the Author

Jenna Capelle lives in Minnesota, also known as the Land of 10,000 Lakes. She enjoys traveling, cooking, practicing yoga, and spending time with family and friends. She received her bachelor of arts degree in public relations and business from Saint Mary's University of Minnesota.

TABLE OF CONTENTS

CHAPTER 1

TALL AND FLAT

Flat land extends as far as the eye can see. Birds sing in the sky above. Then the land drops off. Ground can be seen far below a steep cliff. A river or **valley** sits below the plateau.

 The Ustyurt Plateau is in central Asia.

A plateau is a flat, raised landform. It rises high above the area around it. At least one side of a plateau is steep.

Plateaus are found on every **continent** on Earth. They cover much of Earth's surface. Plateaus can also exist in the ocean. These are called oceanic plateaus.

FUN FACT

In plateau regions, rivers form waterfalls as they fall over steep slopes.

 Niagara Falls is in a plateau region
between the United States and Canada.

CHAPTER 2

BUILDING A PLATEAU

There are three types of plateaus.
Tectonic plates form each type.
These plates make up Earth's
crust. They sit on top of the
mantle. The plates are always
moving. But they move very slowly.

 The Cockburn Range is part of a plateau region in Australia.

Sometimes tectonic plates crash into one another. This takes many years. One plate moves on top of the other. This land is higher than the surrounding area. A plateau forms. This process is known as crustal shortening. The process creates mountains, too.

FUN FACT

The Mascarene Plateau is in the Indian Ocean. It can be seen from space. This plateau covers approximately 770 square miles (2,000 sq km).

 The Waterberg Plateau in Namibia was created by crustal shortening.

Other plateaus form because of thermal expansion. Sometimes an area of mantle is heated quickly.

11

Hot magma comes up toward the crust. But it doesn't break through Earth's surface. Instead, the crust is pushed up. When this happens, a plateau forms. This type of plateau is often flat on top.

Volcanoes can cause plateaus to form, too. Many small eruptions happen over time. Sometimes a **lava flow** happens after the eruptions. The lava spreads over long distances. It builds up over time. Eventually, a plateau

 The North Island Volcanic Plateau in New Zealand has three active volcanoes on it.

forms. This process is called lava

flow generation.

THE TIBETAN PLATEAU

The Tibetan Plateau is the largest plateau in the world. It is in the countries of China, India, Nepal, and Bhutan. This plateau is four times the size of Texas. Some people call it "the rooftop of the world." It is approximately 14,700 feet (4,500 m) high.

The Tibetan Plateau formed 55 million years ago. Two tectonic plates crashed into each other. Over time, the crust lifted straight up. A wide, flat area was formed. This collision also created the Himalayas. This is a huge mountain range. Mount Everest is a part of it.

The Tibetan Plateau is home to animals such as yaks.

CHAPTER 3

MOVING AND CHANGING

Some plateaus move slightly year after year. As the tectonic plates shift, so do plateaus. Plateaus can also grow. The plates continue to crash together over time. This makes the rock push up higher.

The Colorado Plateau is home to the Grand Canyon.

 The Columbia River erodes the Columbia Plateau.

The Colorado Plateau is one example. For millions of years, it has been rising approximately 0.01 inches (0.03 cm) per year.

Plateaus are higher than their surrounding area. This means **erosion** happens often. Erosion from wind or water can shorten or change the shape of a plateau.

Water is the strongest type of erosion. Rivers erode rock. Moving water carries away the **sediment**.

FUN FACT

The Colorado River runs through the Colorado Plateau. It carved the Grand Canyon. This process took millions of years.

Over time, the moving water carves into the plateau. This can form valleys and canyons.

Wind erodes plateaus, too. It blows sediment away from the top. This can make a plateau smaller. It can also change the plateau's shape.

FUN FACT

As plateaus wear down, they can become arches or hoodoos. Hoodoos look like columns. Utah is known for having these landforms.

Cappadocia, Turkey, has hoodoos. They form when wind or water erodes a plateau.

However, the tops of many plateaus are covered with caprock. This type of rock is strong and hard. It helps keep the plateaus from eroding.

CHAPTER 4

LIFE ON A PLATEAU

Many animals and plants live on plateaus. The Putorana Plateau is in Russia. It has more than 7,000 square miles (18,130 sq km) of wilderness. Many plants and animals thrive in this area.

The Kutamarakan River runs through the Putorana Plateau.

Waterfalls and lakes can be found there. Birds visit these sources of water when they migrate. Reindeer pass through these areas, too.

Humans also live on plateaus. People use some plateaus for **agriculture**. Low plateaus are good for farming. High plateaus are good

FUN FACT

The Mato Grosso Plateau is in Brazil. It has forests and grasslands. Many people in this region raise cattle.

 The Atacama Plateau is home to vicuñas. These animals are related to llamas.

for raising livestock. The Atacama Plateau is in Argentina. The land there is not good for growing food.

Instead, people there raise sheep and llamas. They sell the animals' skins and wool.

However, not all plateaus can easily support life. Sometimes plateaus are very high. They have harsh conditions. Many of these plateaus are deserts. For example,

FUN FACT

The Kimberley Plateau region is in Australia. People raise cattle there. They also grow rice, sugarcane, and other crops.

▷ **The central Negev plateau is dry and hot.**

the central Negev plateau is in a
desert in Israel. Plants and animals
have a hard time surviving there.

FOCUS ON
PLATEAUS

Write your answers on a separate piece of paper.

1. Write a sentence that describes the main idea of Chapter 2.

2. If you visited a plateau, what would you be most excited to see? Why?

3. What type of erosion is strongest?
   - **A.** wind erosion
   - **B.** soil erosion
   - **C.** water erosion

4. Why do some plateaus resist erosion?
   - **A.** because there is lots of wind and rain in the area
   - **B.** because their tops are made of hard rock
   - **C.** because people use the plateaus for farming

5. What does **livestock** mean in this book?

*Low plateaus are good for farming. High plateaus are good for raising **livestock**.*

    A. farm animals
    B. plants that people eat
    C. hard rocks

6. What does **migrate** mean in this book?

*Birds visit these sources of water when they **migrate**. Reindeer pass through these areas, too.*

    A. to hunt for food
    B. to move from one area to another
    C. to sleep at night

Answer key on page 32.

GLOSSARY

agriculture
The science of farming animals or plants.

continent
One of the seven large pieces of land on Earth.

crust
Earth's hard outer layer.

erosion
The act of wearing away a surface.

lava flow
Melted rock that spreads over the land following a volcanic eruption.

mantle
The area under the Earth's crust made up of magma and rock.

sediment
Stones, sand, or other materials that are carried by flowing water, wind, or ice.

tectonic plates
Massive pieces of rock that make up Earth's crust.

valley
A low area of land between hills.

TO LEARN MORE

BOOKS

Duke, Shirley. *Erosion*. Vero Beach, FL: Rourke Publishing, 2014.

Lindeen, Mary. *Landforms*. Chicago: Norwood House, 2017.

Rice, William B. *Landforms*. Huntington Beach, CA: Teacher Created Materials, 2014.

NOTE TO EDUCATORS

Visit **www.focusreaders.com** to find lesson plans, activities, links, and other resources related to this title.

INDEX

Answer Key: 1. Answers will vary; **2.** Answers will vary; **3.** C; **4.** B; **5.** A; **6.** B